A Cheese Press History Presents
Veins of Civilization
ANCIENT HISTORY
Book One

BY JORDAN HERMITT
& ANDREA HERMITT

A CHEESE PRESS HISTORY book
Published by Cheese Press Publishing

Copyright © 2024 by Jordan Hermitt & Andrea Hermitt
All rights reserved.

No part of this publication may be reproduced, distributed, or transmitted in any form or by any means, including photocopying, recording, or other electronic or mechanical methods, without the prior written permission of the publisher, except as permitted by U.S. copyright law. For permission requests, contact Cheese Press Publishing.

ISBN: 979-8-89136-006-8

Book Cover by Mere Jones

First Print Edition, August 2024

Cheese Press, LLC
100 Mill Street
Suite A
Lawrenceville, GA 30046

www.CheesePressPublishing.com

This four-year labor of love is a testament to an enduring fascination with the ancient world.

-Andrea Hermitt

Forward

Welcome to a Cheese Press History, collection one. This is the first of a four-year intensive history curriculum with language arts integration. We start with Ancient History, where we know nothing and everything is speculation. That was a joke… Well, MOSTLY a joke.

Each book has four chapters, each designed to be studied one per week, for a total of thirty-two weeks. You will study eight books in total to complete the series. Book one of Ancient History, which you have in your hand right now, is the beginning of this curriculum. If you have not read "An Introduction to the Study of History," you should go back and read that first. While we intend that you study these eight books in chronological order, each chapter could serve as a stand-alone unit study, if you choose. While using the books out of order may cause some loss of context, your typical history buff can make the connections. If you are not already a history enthusiast, you will benefit from doing the program in order.

Language Arts… But isn't this a history book?

Studying literature and history together offers a rich educational experience due to their complementary nature. They work well together. Literature reflects the cultural, social, and historical context of a time period, providing a deeper understanding of societal norms, values, and conflicts. Through literature, we get to experience what life was like in different time periods, informing us of what people thought, what was important to them, and what their problems were. Studying literature alongside history also shows us how cultures change over time offering a holistic view of cultural evolution.

When we connect literature and history, we improve our thinking and analysis skills. Exposure to literature from different historical periods fosters cultural sensitivity and empathy, promoting a more inclusive worldview. Grammar and writing will also be closely integrated into this course. The goal is to enhance writing and communication skills, so that students can articulate thoughts and arguments effectively.

Overall, our goal in combining literature, grammar, and writing into the history course is to make historical events relatable through characters and stories, making them more memorable. We hope that by combining the study of literature and history students will have a more rich and enjoyable learning experience.

Grammar... we know, we know!

At the end of each chapter, we provide a simplified explanation of grammar concepts that track along with the language arts curriculum. This course of study will introduce the basics of grammar that will help you become a better communicator.

Lesson One - An Introduction

Speculation:

- Write down the first five words that come to mind when you think of Ancient History.

_____
_____
_____
_____

- Describe the longest period of time that you can think of.

_____
_____
_____
_____

- How do you think about or divvy up different time periods of your childhood?

_____
_____
_____
_____
_____

Understanding the Ancient Ages

History is generally split up into different eras, periods, ages, dynasties, etc. The use of these terms are dependent on country and region, though many of them also overlap. For example, the **Stone Age** is a larger umbrella term that covers different eras nestled within the time period we will be discussing.

The Stone Age is a predecessor to what is known as the **Metal Ages**. This may seem confusing since stone and metal both come out of the ground, but at the same time, stones and metals are classified as different compounds, and the process we use to turn them into tools is also different. None of this rambling truly matters, though, since no one writing this book is making significant historical or scientific distinctions on this point. So for future reference, the Stone Age is pre-Metal Ages

Stone Age: dates from about two million BCE to about 3,500 BCE. This is the umbrella term that covers several different ages of history within it. Initially this is the stage of human culture when stone tools and weapons were made and used.

Metal Ages: Periods of drastic change due to technological innovation in the 3rd, 2nd, and 1st millennium BCE.

Delineation: a precise description detailing the differences between that being described and other things.

but we're going to talk about them together. Back on topic, the Metal Ages are **delineations** in changes of technology.

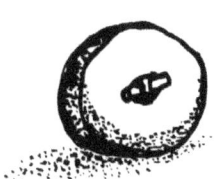

We are currently discussing the Stone Age, but there are also the Bronze Age, Iron Age, and Copper Ages. The Stone Age houses three distinct periods, the **Paleolithic**, **Mesolithic**, and **Neolithic** periods. The Paleolithic period (aka the Old Stone Age) is the earliest chunk of the Stone Age, spanning from roughly 2.5 million years ago to 10,000 BCE. This chunk of history coincides with the earliest evidence of Homo genus activity. Technically, there are even smaller sub-categories of the Paleolithic period: lower, middle, and upper. However, due to people doing different stuff in different places at different times, these aren't as well defined. The Mesolithic, or Middle Stone Age, doesn't show many technological advancements, but it does show adaptations in cultural regions.

Paleolithic: The time from 2 million years BCE until 12,000 BCE. Also called the Old Stone Age (Britannica, 2024).

Mesolithic: "The Mesolithic Period, or Middle Stone Age, is an archaeological term describing specific cultures that fall between the Paleolithic and the Neolithic Periods. While the start and end dates of the Mesolithic Period vary by geographical region, it dated approximately from 10,000 BCE to 8,000 BCE." (Boundless.com, n.d.)

Neolithic: "The Neolithic Period, also called the New Stone Age, is the final stage of cultural evolution or technological development among prehistoric humans." (Britannica,, 2023) from around 8,000-4,500 BCE

That sentence doesn't seem like it means anything, but here's the thing: the Mesolithic period happened after a significant amount of migration. This means that any advancements that were made during this time were being discovered apart from each other. This was a time of technique adaptation, cultural development, and diversity.

Rabbit Trail: There are several theories about human migration. While we will discuss it more later, feel free to dig into the topic on your own.

Stratification: The classification of items into different groups.

The Neolithic period, or Late Stone Age period, is all about further cultural development and **stratification**. This is when people were finally developing skills that allowed them to settle in a singular location and establish tribe-like settlements. Unlike the turn from the Paleolithic Period to the Mesolithic Period, the turn from the Mesolithic Period to the Neolithic is a pretty

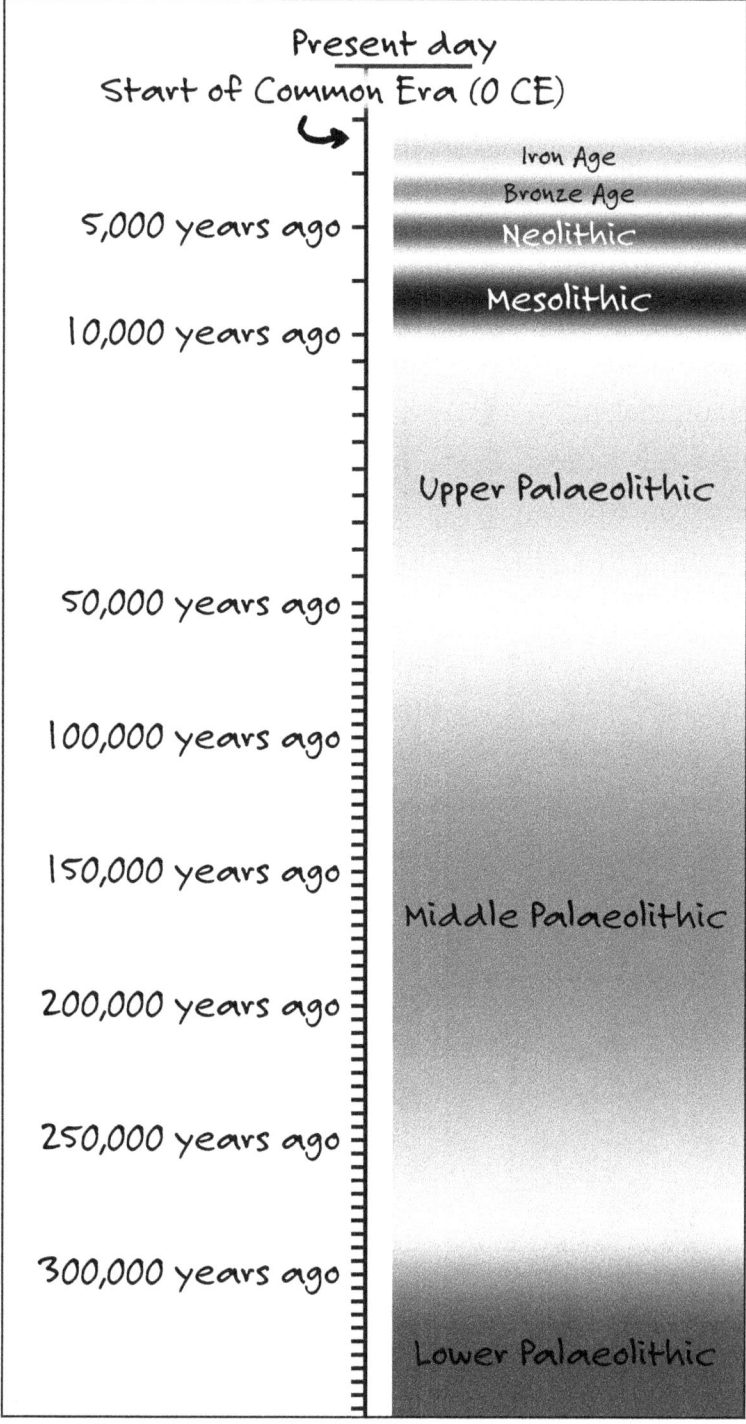

Neolithic Revolution: The wide-scale transition of many human cultures during the Neolithic period from a lifestyle of hunting and gathering to one of agriculture and settlement, making an increasingly large population possible.

dramatic one. In fact, it was so dramatic that it was given a title: **The Neolithic Revolution**.

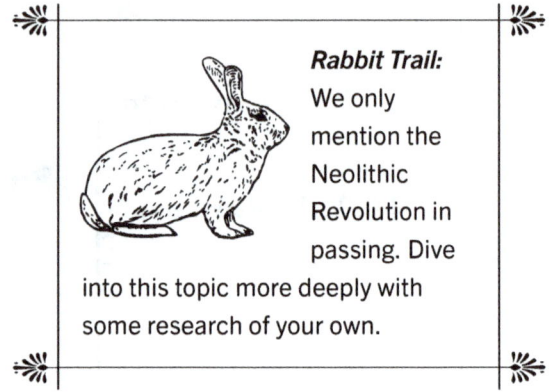

Rabbit Trail: We only mention the Neolithic Revolution in passing. Dive into this topic more deeply with some research of your own.

The **Copper Age**, also known as the Chalcolithic Age, is a big name for an age that no one mentions more than they have to, and when they do, they generally don't call it that. The Copper Age is kind of a filler period between the end of the Neolithic period and the beginning of the Bronze Age, which happened around the mid-5th millennium BCE until either the late 4th or 3rd millennium BCE, depending upon region.

The Bronze Age spans from approximately 3,300 BCE to 1,200 BCE, depending on geographical location. Behold, people have begun to work with metal! This is also the beginning of not only civilizations but

Foundation figure of king Shulgi of Ur, carrying a basket. The Met Museum. Public Domain.

also organized government. There are several major Bronze Age civilizations, such as Ancient Egypt, Ancient China, Indus River Valley, Mycenaean Greece (not to be mistaken with Ancient Greece), Ancient Europe, and the Middle East. Keep in mind that each of these regions experienced the same advancements, but all at different times over the course of 2000 years.

The Iron Age is generally from 1,200 BCE to 600 BCE once again, depending on where you are. **Counterintuitively**, the Iron Age didn't take off because of the advent of iron. It was not until people understood how to make **alloys** and turn iron into steel, which allowed them to make specific tools and weapons, that this age really started. The Iron Age brought widespread improvements to people's lives in terms of the tools they were using. These humans weren't extremely physically different from their predecessors, however, they were exponentially more effective. This age is all about the quality of the tools. Higher-quality tools make doing hard jobs easier, impossible jobs possible, and every job faster. This then also

Copper Age: An early phase of the Bronze Age, a transitional age between the Stone Age and Bronze Age around 3,500 BCE.

Counterintuitively: Anything that is different or opposite from what you would expect.

Alloy: Any homogeneous metal mixture composed of two or more metal, nonmetal, or metalloid elements. For example steel is an alloy of iron and carbon.

freed up time that was previously spent just trying to survive for people to do pretty much anything else, which the vast majority of the population never had a chance to do before. Imagine suddenly, after having to spend all your time surviving, being able to pick up a hobby or just take a nap and not having it mean that you and your family would starve.

These ages are the main way we talk about time in BCE. This doesn't cover all the different dynasties, periods, and eras that will pop up within these Metal Ages, but we'll be sure to talk about those as they come. To complicate this further, the time span between approximately 2.4 million BCE and 11,500 BCE was the last **Ice Age**. During this time, the climate would fluctuate abruptly; in fact, it did so approximately 25 times (Schmidt & Hertzberg, 2011). These warming and cooling shifts occurred swiftly, and when we say swiftly, we mean over the course of a couple of decades, which is really quick for climate shifts. These shifts cause interesting migration patterns that we'll begin discussing

Ice Age: An ice age is a period of colder global temperatures and recurring glacial expansion capable of lasting hundreds of millions of years.

Hunter Gatherer Culture: A basic existence way of living that relies on hunting, fishing, and foraging for wild plants and animals (National Geographic Society, 2024).

The Land Bridge Theory: The land bridge theory proposes that early human migrations occurred across a now-submerged land connection, known as the Bering Land Bridge, which emerged during periods of lower sea levels, allowing passage between northeastern Asia and northwestern North America. This theory suggests that such migrations played a crucial role in populating the Americas during prehistoric times (United States National Park Service, 2023)

in the future chapters. These conditions were not conducive to settlement. Especially given the fact that people had yet to figure out, or lacked the capacity to understand, agriculture at the time. So, early people lived in a **hunter-gatherer culture**.

Before we can completely move on from the Ice Age, we have to mention the **Land Bridge Theory**. This theory, proposed in the 1590's by French missionary Fray Jose de Acosta, is the working theory on how people migrated to the Americas. The theory presumes that during this time there were lower sea levels due to a lot of water being ice, which would have allowed people to walk from Asia to the Americas. In recent years, this theory has begun to be questioned and challenged more and more by new research. We will discuss this further in upcoming chapters.

 Watch this Video: How Historians Measure Time
http://link.cheesepresspublishing.com/measureTime

Literature: Historical Fiction

Historical fiction is a literary genre that combines elements of history and fiction, using real historical events, settings, and figures as a backdrop for fictional stories. It allows authors to explore and interpret the past, providing readers with a unique perspective on historical events while offering an engaging narrative. Key aspects of historical fiction include setting in a specific time and place, blending fact and fiction, researching historical context, exploring universal themes, character development, and providing an immersive reading experience. Authors invest significant time and effort in research, studying primary sources and historical documents, and immersing themselves in the culture of the period. This genre often explores universal themes, such as love, conflict, power, and identity, and can comment on contemporary issues by drawing parallels between historical events and contemporary concerns. Historical fiction is a broad genre that includes various subgenres, such as Medieval, Renaissance, Regency, World War I and II, and more, allowing for exploration of different historical periods and cultural contexts.

THE CAVE BOY OF THE AGE OF STONE BY MARGARET A. McINTYRE

CHAPTER VI: THE COMING OF FIRE

When Strongarm came back from the hunt, he found the cave cold and dark and wet. A stream of water was running down through the smoke-hole. It had put out the fire. The ashes, too, were wet; and there were no coals from which to start the fire again.

He looked at the black fire-place.

"Now I must walk all the way to old Hickory's for fire," he grumbled, "and it is growing dark."

Tired and hungry, he left the cave.

He had not gone far when a dead branch fell across his path. He jumped back.

"The people who live in the trees did that—some of those shadow people," he said to himself. "They tried to kill me. The man who lives in the wind is angry, too. Hear him roar!

"I do not like shadow people," he thought as he walked on. "They live in trees and wind and rivers and fire and stones and everything, but you cannot see them. They will hurt you if you make them angry. I am afraid of them. I wish I had a torch to scare them off. All the other shadow people are afraid of the fire man."

Then to keep up his heart he sang in a loud gruff voice:

"O why did the water put out the fire?

O why did the water put out the fire?"

Strongarm gave a loud call as he came up to Hickory's cave. The old man came to the door and asked what the trouble was.

"Trouble enough," growled Strongarm. "My fire is out. I came for coals."

Old Hickory gave a great roaring laugh. His wife laughed, too, as she pushed the children aside and raked out coals. These she put into a hollow branch that Strongarm handed her.

"They will keep alive in there," he said, "even if it rains."

Then with a good pine torch and his branch full of coals, he hurried home.

When Burr came back to the cave, she, too, found the fire out. There was a deer on the floor, so she knew that Strongarm had come from the hunt.

"The man has gone to old Hickory's for fire," she told her father.

"Um," said Flint, "he might have rested his legs. I can get fire from stones."

"From stones!" cried Burr, her face white.

The old man quietly pulled two stones from his bag. One was flint, the other was quartz. He took dry leaves from his bag and rubbed them very fine between his hands and laid them on a rock. Over the leaves he held the two stones and began to strike one with the other.

Burr and the boys watched with scared faces.

"The fire man—will he not be angry?" she asked.

Flint said nothing. He was striking the stones together. A spark came! then another and another! He kept on striking very fast until the sparks came like a flame and caught the dry leaves. He put on more leaves and little sticks, and soon there was a good fire blazing on the floor.

"From stones!" Burr kept thinking, as she shook her head and watched it out of the corner of her eye.

When Strongarm came with the coals, the cave was already warm and light and full of the smell of good things cooking. He looked at the fire and wondered where it had come from, but said nothing.

Near the fire his wife had a basket lined with clay. In it were the seeds of the wild grains and acorns, with hot coals. She shook the basket around and around until the seeds were roasted. Then from the ashes she pulled the roots she had put there to roast.

After Strongarm had eaten, he lay down by the fire. Nodding toward it he said, "Where did you get it?"

Flint then told him that he had brought it out of stones. Strongarm sat up and looked hard at Flint. Then Flint had to strike the stones together again, to let Strongarm see the fire come out.

"Beaver Tail, an old ax maker, showed me how to do it," said Flint. "He has worked in stone all his life. For a long time he has known that fire lives in stone. He has seen sparks fly as he chipped his axes. One day in making a spear head, he struck a quartz pebble with his flint hammer stone. A big spark came! He struck again and again, and the sparks came fast and caught the dry grass at his feet!"

"Um," grunted Strongarm, wondering. He thought for a long time; then he looked at Flint and said, "Fire lives in wood, too! My ax handles grow warm as I rub them."

The boys listened in wonder to their grandfather's strange story of the making of fire.

After a time Thorn said, "We have always had fire in the cave. All the cave folks have it. They did not bring it from stones. Where did they get it?"

"Once, in the old days," Strongarm said, and turned to the boy, "a man saw fire come out of the sky and begin to eat up the woods! He could feel the fire from where he stood. It made him warm, and he liked it. But he was afraid to take any, for he thought the fire man might be angry. But at last he did take some. He kept it, and grew to like it more and more. With it burning beside him, the night was not so dark, and he was not afraid, for the hungry wolf and tiger turned away—teeth and claws could not fight fire!

"The other men saw that it was good to have fire; so, in time, they took some of it. And ever since then, every man has tried to keep his fire burning."

"It is better for us cave folks since fire came," Burr then said, nodding to the boys. "Why, before it came, there was no cooked meat, nor were there any sweet roasted seeds or roots. But the folks tore their meat from the animal where it was killed, and stood by and ate it raw.

"Nor was there a home before fire came. My grandmother told me that, long ago, in the old days, the men and women wandered from place to place with their little children. And the women hunted and fished and fought beside the men. And at night the people curled themselves round as the wild dogs do, and slept on the ground; and the rain wet them, and the cold winds made them shiver.

"But after fire came, all this was changed. For the fire would go out unless there was someone to keep it. So a man told his wife that she might stay and keep the fire, and said that he would hunt for both.

"The woman then took a place that she liked, near a stream, and built a shelter of branches and made her fire there and kept it. And the man brought meat to her, and she cooked it. And before very long all the people were living in that way. And so ever since that time, the man has been the hunter, and the woman has kept the fire and brought water from the stream and gathered seeds of the ripe grasses."

"And always since then, too, the family place has been about the fire. We sit beside it and warm ourselves and work and talk and rest; and that is home."

"True, true," grunted old Flint; and Strongarm nodded his head.

‖O‖O‖O‖O‖O‖O‖O‖O‖O‖O‖O‖O‖O‖O‖O‖O‖O‖O‖O‖O‖O‖O‖O‖O‖O‖O‖O‖O‖O‖O‖O‖O‖O‖O‖O‖O‖

Read the full story

Online: http://link.cheesepresspublishing.com/caveBoy

Kindle: https://amzn.to/3RLTKvK

Grammar: Nouns, Articles, and Adjectives

Nouns

Nouns are words that name people, places, things, or ideas.

Here are some examples:

- **People:** Words like "scientist," and "human," are nouns because they name people.
- **Places:** Words like "cave," and "region," are nouns because they name places.
- **Things:** Words like "stone," "metal," and "ice" are nouns because they name things you can see and touch.
- **Ideas:** Words like "time," "leisure," and "category" are nouns because they name feelings or concepts.

You can usually tell if a word is a noun if it answers the questions "Who?" or "What?"

- Who researches ancient ruins? (Answer: "an archeologist" - a noun)
- What were the first things humans created? (Answer: "tools" - a noun)
- What is a division of ancient time? (Answer: "an age" - a noun).

Nouns can also be common or proper

- Common nouns are general names for things (like "rock" or "ax").
- Proper nouns are specific names and always start with a capital letter (like "Strongarm" for a character's name, or "Egypt" for a country).

As you can see, nouns are important because they help us name and talk about the world around us!

Articles

Articles are words that are typically used before nouns. They help to specify whether the noun is something specific or general. There are two types of articles: definite and indefinite.

Definite Article: "The"

- **"The"** is used when talking about a specific person, place, thing, or idea that both the speaker and listener know about.

    Example: "The fire burned brightly." (This refers to a specific fire that both the speaker and listener know about.)

Indefinite Articles: "A" and "An"

- **"A"** and **"An"** are used when talking about something general or not specific.
    - Use "A" before words that start with a consonant sound.

        Example: "A man is sitting by the fire." (This refers to any man, not a specific one.)

    - Use "An" before words that start with a vowel sound.

        Example: "An ax was used to cut the firewood." (This refers to any ax, not a specific one.)

Adjectives

An adjective is a word that describes a noun. Adjectives give more information about the noun, making sentences more interesting and detailed.

- **Describing People:**

    "The early humans moved because the weather got cold."

    "Early" is an adjective describing the humans.

- **Describing Places:**

    "The archeologist studied the ancient ruins."

    "Ancient" is an adjective describing the ruins.

- **Describing Things:**

    "The people gathered around the warm fire."

    "Warm" is an adjective describing the fire.

- **Describing Ideas:**

    "The archeologist discovered a Bronze Age tool."

    "Bronze" is an adjective describing the age.
    Note: an adjective can be part of a proper noun.

Adjectives can tell us:

- What kind: "dark cave," "sharp ax"
- Which one: "this age," "that ruin"
- How many: "three tools," "few records"
- How much: "enough water," "long time"

Using adjectives makes your sentences more colorful and helps people get a clearer picture of what you're talking about.

Contemplation: *(please answer questions in depth- answers would be 100 words or more)*

- How do scientists differentiate between Paleolithic, Mesolithic, and Neolithic periods? What makes each period unique?

- How did the Metal Ages change life for early people?

- Watch the "How We Study History" video. Pick one historical fact in the chapter and find 3 sources that back up the stated fact. Provide the pertinent text, and link, or other source information.

References

Schmidt, M. W. & Hertzberg, J. E. (2011) Abrupt Climate Change During the Last Ice Age. *Nature Education Knowledge* 3(10):11 https://www.nature.com/scitable/knowledge/library/abrupt-climate-change-during-the-last-ice-24288097/

Britannica, T. Editors of Encyclopaedia (2023, June 23). *Neolithic.* Encyclopedia Britannica. https://www.britannica.com/event/Neolithic

Britannica, T. Editors of Encyclopaedia (2024, May 22). *Paleolithic Period.* Encyclopedia Britannica. https://www.britannica.com/event/Paleolithic-Period

Boundless.com (Ed.). (n.d.). Course hero. *Boundless Art History: Mesolithic Art.* https://courses.lumenlearning.com/boundless-arthistory/chapter/the-mesolithic-period

The Bering Land Bridge Theory. (2023, June 21). Bering Land Bridge National Preserve (U.S. National Park Service). https://www.nps.gov/bela/learn/historyculture/the-bering-land-bridge-theory.htm

Foundation figure of king Shulgi of Ur, carrying a basket. (ca. 2094-2047 BCE). The Metropolitain Museum of Art. https://www.metmuseum.org/art/collection/search/324831

National Geographic Society (2024, February 9). *Encyclopedia Entry: Hunter-Gatherer Culture* https://education.nationalgeographic.org/resource/hunter-gatherer-culture/

Lesson Two - People

Speculation:

- What do you think of when you hear the words "ancient technology"?

_____
_____
_____

- When have you found a new use for something intended for another purpose?

_____
_____
_____

- What do you know about the creation of the world?

_____
_____
_____
_____
_____

Ancient Humans

Cave Painting Handprints. Licensed by Adobe Stock.

Long long ago, there were people… or so we assume. Obviously, humans happened eventually, but there's quite a few where's, when's, and how's to consider when thinking about the beginning of the world and humanity. From a historical perspective, we have many stories about how a culture or humanity came to be, but that's for a later time. For now, we're going to stick with the idea that, at some point in history, people did appear. We know this to be true, as you are currently here reading this book. When did this happen? Not sure, but we can start theorizing.

Approx. 2,500,000 BCE

The furthest back we can date **fossils** of what we currently consider full human skeletons, **Homo sapiens**, is about 2.5 million years ago. There were other and earlier bipedal humanoid species that belonged to the Homo **genus**, however, the emergence of Homo sapiens is the beginning of what we consider human beings. We call this time period, before written records, the **Prehistoric Era** or **prehistory**

Fossils: The petrified or preserved remains of prehistoric organisms.

Homo sapiens: The species of humankind.

Genus: A biological classification of similar species.

Prehistoric Era (Prehistory): The designation of the period of time before written records.

Cave Painting Human Figures. Licensed by Adobe Stock.

(ironic for a history book). This time period spans across a multitude of historical eras up until around 5,000 years ago.

Though we know people were around 2.5 million years ago, we don't get proof of people "peopling" (like using tools, standing erect, you know... doing people stuff) until several hundred thousand years later.

Approx. 2,400,000 BCE

Throughout its existence, the Earth has periodically gone through **glaciation** periods, better known as Ice Ages. The earliest one we know about is called the Huronian glacial period which spanned from around 2.4 million years ago to about 2.1 million years ago. We know this based on the rare geological specimen we have from this period (Earle & Earle, 2015).

Glaciers. Licensed by Adobe Stock.

Approx. 2,100,000 BCE

We find proof of human existence at the Olduvai Gorge in what is now Modern Tanzania, Africa. The findings from this archaeological site date back to the Stone Age, more specifically a subsection of the Stone Age called the Paleolithic Age (or Early Stone Age), which is where we find the earliest human activity. What we do know about early human activity during this period is that they were existing in a hunter/gatherer culture.

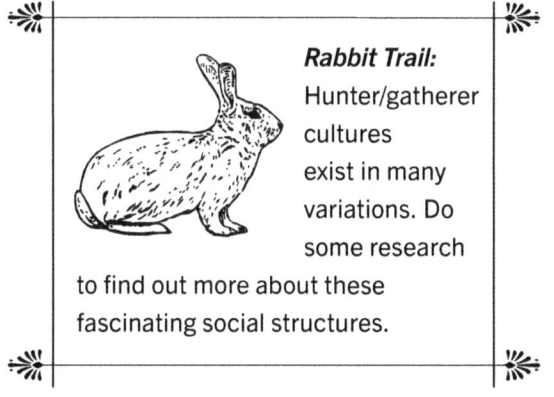

Rabbit Trail: Hunter/gatherer cultures exist in many variations. Do some research to find out more about these fascinating social structures.

Olduvai Gorge **artifacts** can be dated back to 2.1 million years ago. The collection of bones and artifacts found at this site sparked scientific debate about early human behavior and activity. The findings in Olduvai Gorge not only show the earliest evidence of human activity, but it also shows the adaptability of early people as they adjusted to the

Glaciation: The buildup of Ice across the Earth's surface.

Artifacts: An object made by a person, tools, or ornaments that show pieces of the past.

constant changing of the environment. The oldest stone tools found here are from a culture that archaeologists call the Oldowan. This site shows how early humans interacted with their surroundings in new ways, such as developing new ways to consume food that combined meat and plants. The concentration of stone tools and animal fossils shows that both humans as well as animals gathered near water sources. There is also evidence that Oldowan people looked in many places for food and water. The research indicates that early humans transported rocks with them that they collected from far away places and used as tools. They also learned how to adapt to different environments (Ellwood & Williams, 2008). Speaking of human activity, about 1.5 million years ago in India there was another hub of human activity (Florin, 2022).

Approx. 1,500,000 BCE

In not so human news, this was around the same time **Homo erectus** emerged. Remember those other genuses of people? Similar to modern humans, they stood upright and used tools. They are similar to but genetically distinct from Homo-sapiens. They had shorter arms and longer legs in proportion to their torsos. Due to their skull shape, they most likely had smaller brains and may have been less intelligent. However, with their ability to stand upright, an ability they gained sooner than Homo sapiens, they were able to make technological strides more quickly than we did. They also seem to be the first people to migrate out of Africa (Hendry, n.d.).

The Attirampakkam archaeological site in Southeast India has something new, tools! Well, not entirely new... Olduvai also had tools but Attirampakkam had the oldest tools... which is something. Archaeologists found the oldest **Acheulean tools**, dating back to somewhere between 1 and 1.7 million years old at this site. Acheulean tools are characterized by extremely versatile handaxes in pear, teardrop, and rounded shapes used for a variety of chores. These tools were likely made by Homo erectus. Moving from tools to technology, fire began to be used around 1.4 million years ago.

Homo erectus: An extinct species similar to Homo sapiens.

Acheulean Tools: A method of tool creation used to make a stone tool in a characteristic tear drop shape.

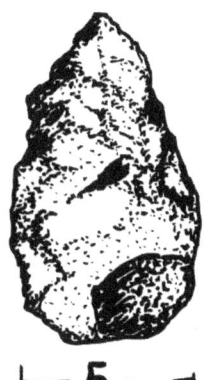

⊢ 5 cm ⊣
(on average)

Approx. 1,400,000 BCE

Yes, fire is technology. It doesn't sound like much but imagine not being able to cook your food or have light at night then suddenly being able to do both of those things. I'm sure early Homo species thought it was awesome. Now, this isn't the "discovery" of fire. At several points before this, people had seen the aftermath of lightning hitting a tree or something. However, we don't find evidence of fire being harnessed until about 14 million years ago around the Lake Turkana region of Kenya. Koobi Fora, a region of Lake Turkana, had oxidized patches of earth several centimeters deep which scholars interpret as signs of controlled fire, such as bonfires or fire pits. This is the earliest proof of controlled fire and only within a small region.

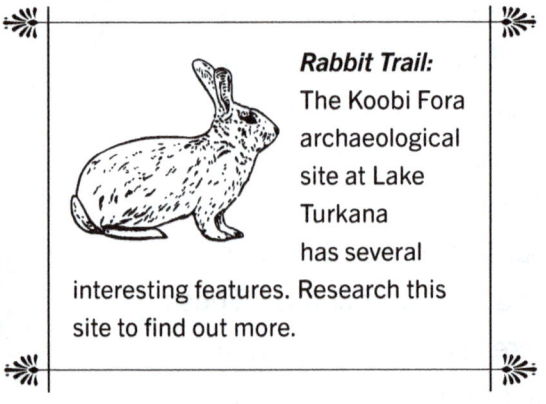

Rabbit Trail: The Koobi Fora archaeological site at Lake Turkana has several interesting features. Research this site to find out more.

600,000 BCE

Around six hundred thousand years ago is when people began to really spread out for the first time. Migration took people from a more centralized point in

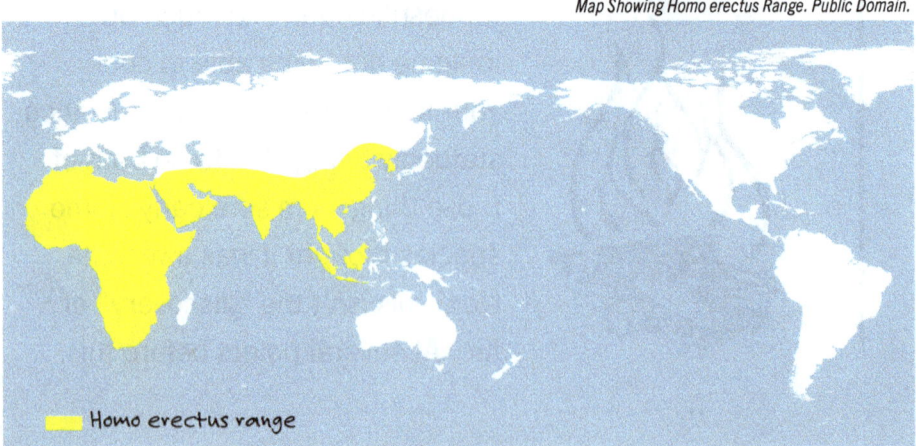

Map Showing Homo erectus Range. Public Domain.

Africa and out into the rest of the continent into Asia and Europe. This was once again mostly Homo erectus spreading and because of this their population was able to expand to around 1.5 million (Gibbons, 2019) (Hendry, n.d.).

As people began to settle in different regions of the world, they began to make new forms of tools.

Approx. 420,000 BCE

In the area of Essex, England, people created a spear. This was a lethal, close ranged weapon carved by flint tools. It was discovered at Clacton-on-Sea in Essex, England, during excavations in 1911. The Clacton Spear is considered one of the oldest wooden tools ever found. It is made from yew wood and measures about 38 centimeters (15 inches) in length. It has a pointed tip and a sharpened edge, indicating that it was likely used as a hunting or cutting tool (Warren, n.d.).

400,000 BCE

The Acheulean handaxe, was made from an iconic and distinctive type of prehistoric stone which existed during the Lower Paleolithic period. It

was likely made and used by **Neanderthals**. It was first found in France in the mid-19th century, and named after the site of Saint-Acheul which was active around 400,000 BCE. These were not the first Acheulean tools made, just the first ones we found. If this tool sounds familiar, it is because we mentioned it earlier as the oldest Acheulean handaxe, which was found in India (Corbey et.al., 2016).

> **Neanderthals:** An extinct species similar to Homo sapiens.
>
> **Flint:** A type of hard gray rock that chips easily and easily produces sparks.

The Acheulean handaxe was produced using a method called bifacial reduction, where stone knappers systematically shape the core by removing flakes from both sides until the desired form is achieved. It is a versatile tool with a symmetrical design, shaped through flaking on both sides, providing functional advantages. Its teardrop or oval shape allows for a comfortable grip making it a multi-purpose tool. It was effective for cutting, chopping, hunting, and butchering tasks.

300,000 BCE

There is no evidence that stone spear heads were used until 200,000 BCE. However, in Morocco there have been **flint** blades found in the remnants of fire near the skeletons of Homo sapiens. Flint blades being left or dropped during travel are good evidence of migration (Metcalfe, 2020) (Agam, et al., 2020).

So far, we've given you a bunch of information and broad dates concerning evidence of people... peopling. Which, at this time, is mostly just the active pursuit of not dying. This is meant to give you a main overview of the very early whats and whens of human activity. In the next chapter, we'll be going over the hows and whys that shape the progression of human behavior.

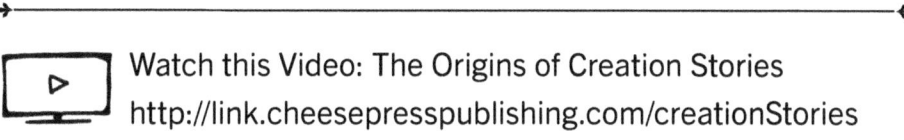

Watch this Video: The Origins of Creation Stories
http://link.cheesepresspublishing.com/creationStories

Literature: Creation Stories, Various Authors

Every culture has a creation story. At some point, people started asking, "Where did we come from?" and "How did we get here?" and from this, many origin-of-man stories emerged. At some point or another, most origin stories may have been religiously held beliefs. Even those that seem fantastical to us today.

These creation stories provide explanations for how the world and humans came to be. They specifically answer fundamental questions about the beginnings of life, nature, and the universe. Often, these stories are a key part of a culture's identity. They reflect the values, beliefs, and traditions of a community, helping to unify its members around a common heritage.

Considering how eerily similar these stories are, it seems that the different cultures may have been more connected at some point in time.

Mesopotamian - Enuma Elish

"When in the height heaven was not named, And the earth beneath did not yet bear a name, And the primeval Apsû, who begat them, And chaos, Tiamat, the mother of them both, Their waters were mingled together, And no field was formed, no marsh was to be seen; When of the gods none had been called into being, And none bore a name, and no destinies were ordained; Then were created the gods in the midst of heaven."

Hebrew - Genesis

"In the beginning God created the heavens and the earth. Now the earth was formless and empty, darkness was over the surface of the deep, and the Spirit of God was hovering over the waters. And God said, 'Let there be light,' and there was light."

Hindu - Rigveda

"There was neither non-existence nor existence then; There was neither the realm of space nor the sky which is beyond. What stirred? Where? In whose protection? Was there water, bottomlessly deep? There was neither death nor immortality then. There was no distinguishing sign of night nor of day. That one thing, breathless, breathed by its own nature: Apart from it was nothing whatsoever."

Egyptian - The Memphite Theology

"Before heaven and earth had been created, before men and gods had been born, before death had been created, I alone existed, the god Ptah. And I brought into being all things that are. I thought in my heart, and the thought became a reality. I spoke my word, and it became life. I called the name of everything, and it came to be."

Chinese - Pan Gu and the Creation of the World

"In the beginning, the universe was in a state of chaos, like a chicken's egg, and Pan Gu was born inside it. He grew for eighteen thousand years until he broke through the egg, separating the clear (yang) from the turbid (yin). The clear became the sky, and the turbid became the earth. Pan Gu stood between them and pushed up the sky, which grew taller and taller each day, while the earth became thicker and thicker."

Norse - Völuspá (Poetic Edda)

"In the beginning, there was nothing but the Ginnungagap, the Yawning Void. To the north of the void was the icy realm of Niflheim, and to the south was the fiery realm of Muspelheim. Where the two realms met, the fire melted the ice, and from the drops sprang Ymir, the first of the giants. As Ymir slept, more giants emerged from his sweat, and the primeval cow, Audhumla, was formed from the ice to nourish him."

Pronouns

Pronouns are words used to replace nouns and are often used to refer to people in conversation and writing. It is used to avoid repetition of a noun.

- **Subject pronouns:** perform the action in a sentence Ex: I, you, he, she, it, we, you, they
- **Object pronouns:** receive the action in a sentence Ex: Me, you, him, her, it, us, you, them
- **Possessive Pronouns:** show ownership Ex: Mine, yours, his, hers, its, ours, yours, theirs
- **Reflexive:** used to refer back to the subject in the sentence Ex: myself, yourself, herself, himself, oneself, itself, ourselves, themselves, yourselves
- **Demonstrative Pronouns:** used to point to specific objects Ex: This, these, that, those
- **Interrogative Pronouns:** used to ask questions Ex: who, whom, which, what
- **Relative Pronouns:** used to relate one part of the sentence to another Ex: who, whom, whose, that, which, whoever, whichever, whomever

Pronouns Continued

- **Indefinite Pronouns:** do not refer to any particular person, place or thing Ex: all, another, any, anybody, anyone, anything, each, everybody, everyone, everything, few, many, nobody, none, several, some, somebody, someone

- **Reciprocal Pronouns:** used to express a mutual relationship Ex: each other, one another

- **Personal Pronouns:** used to substitute proper names. Ex: I, you, he, she, we, they, him, her, he, she, us, them

  Note: It is important to understand that 'they' can be singular or plural. It can be used for a group of people, but also for a singular person when the gender is unknown, or doesn't matter in the context.

Contemplation: *(please answer questions in depth- answers would be 100 words or more)*

- What kinds of evidence do you think scientists use to learn about ancient humans?

- How did tools and technology change the lives of ancient people?

- Choose one of the archaeological sites discussed in this chapter and find three sources that tell you more about this site. Provide the pertinent text, links, or other source information.

References

Agam, A., Wilson, L., Gopher, A. et al. (2020 Dec). Flint Type Analysis of Bifaces From Acheulo-Yabrudian Qesem Cave (Israel) Suggests an Older Acheulian Origin. *J Paleo Arch 3*, pp. 719–754. https://doi.org/10.1007/s41982-019-00038-0

Corbey, R., Jagich, A., Vaesen, K., & Collard, M. (2016). The Acheulean handaxe: More like a bird's song than a beatles' tune?. *Evolutionary anthropology, 25*(1), 6–19. https://doi.org/10.1002/evan.21467

Earle, S., & Earle, S. (2015, September 1). *16.1 glacial periods in Earth's history.* Physical Geology. https://opentextbc.ca/geology/chapter/16-1-glacial-periods-in-earths-history/

Ellwood, C. A., & Williams, D. P. (2008). University of Missouri. *Oldowan and Acheulean Stone Tools* | Museum of Anthropology - Museum of Anthropology. https://anthromuseum.missouri.edu/e-exhibits/oldowan-and-acheulean-stone-tools

Florin, J. M. (2022, September 13). *Finds in Tanzania's Olduvai Gorge reveal how ancient humans adapted to change.* The Conversation. https://theconversation.com/finds-in-tanzanias-olduvai-gorge-reveal-how-ancient-humans-adapted-to-change-150755

Gibbons, A. (2019, October 28). *Experts question study claiming to pinpoint birthplace of all humans* - AAAS. Science. https://www.science.org/content/article/experts-question-study-claiming-pinpoint-birthplace-all-humans

Hendry, L. (n.d.). *Homo erectus, our ancient ancestor.* Natural History Museum. https://www.nhm.ac.uk/discover/homo-erectus-our-ancient-ancestor.html

Metcalfe, T. (2020, August 19). *Ancient stone "breadcrumbs" reveal early human migration out of Africa.* LiveScience. https://www.livescience.com/early-humans-out-of-africa-flints.html

Warren, S. H. (n.d.). *Clacton Spear* - Google Arts & Culture. Google. https://artsandculture.google.com/asset/clacton-spear/5AG6e8E0Snoj5g?hl=en

Lesson Three - Human Behavior

Speculation:

- What do you think some considerations would be for life without modern structures?

_____
_____
_____
_____

- What environmental challenges do you think early humans faced, and how might they have adapted to these challenges?

_____
_____
_____
_____

- List some things that would make you permanently leave where you live right now.

_____
_____
_____
_____

Early Paleolithic

Fire. Licensed by Adobe Stock.

It's the early Paleolithic period, and people are... really not doing all that much. What you need to understand is that once society makes an advancement, it gets easier to make new ones. You'll see advancement booms every time people make a really big discovery. However, right now we're still barely past banging rocks together, and we're still figuring out uses for fire. Since we mentioned fire...

164,000 BCE

More uses for fire! Around this time in South Africa, at the Pinnacle Point Site, people began experimenting with heating up **silcrete stone** to make it easier to flake and turn into tools, which was a bit better than the previous smashing method. In fact, at this time, in what is current-day Cape Town, Africa, some of the earliest knives were being chipped and sharpened from stone and then hardened by heating them up with fire. So while it doesn't seem like a lot, and it definitely seems slow, every discovery people make is moving them further toward technological advancements. The chipping method and the harnessing of fire have been

Silcrete Stone: A hardened layer of soil, sand, gravel, and silica that resists crumbling away or powdering.

put together to improve life for early Homo genus people (Hughes, 2009).

133,000 BCE

By this time, people have definitely reached what we currently call Greece. The evidence found at the Theopetra Cave Site seems to indicate that these cave systems were active from the Upper Paleolithic period through the **Pleistocene and Holocene**.

Pleistocene: The earlier half of the Quaternary period immediately prior to the Holocene Epoch (Britannica, 2018).

Holocene: A geological layer of stone that shows the latest interval of geologic time, around the last 11,700 years or the later Quaternary period (Fairbridge & Agenbroad, 2024). We currently live in the Holocene Epoch.

Brue, 1762. Public Domain.

Cave of Theopetra, Image by Claire Cox. Licensed under Creative Commons 2.0 BY-ND.

      Theopetra Cave, located in Thessaly, Greece, is a significant archaeological site with a rich history of human habitation and activities dating back thousands of years. The cave's limestone formation, estimated to be around 130,000 years old, provides valuable insights into the long-term human history of the region. The cave has yielded a wealth of artifacts, tools, and cultural remains, providing insights into the lifestyles, technologies, and adaptations of prehistoric inhabitants. The cave also contributes significantly to our understanding of human evolution and cultural development in the Mediterranean region. The cave is divided into several archaeological phases, providing a detailed chronology of human occupation. The sediment layers in the cave have preserved artifacts and environmental evidence, allowing

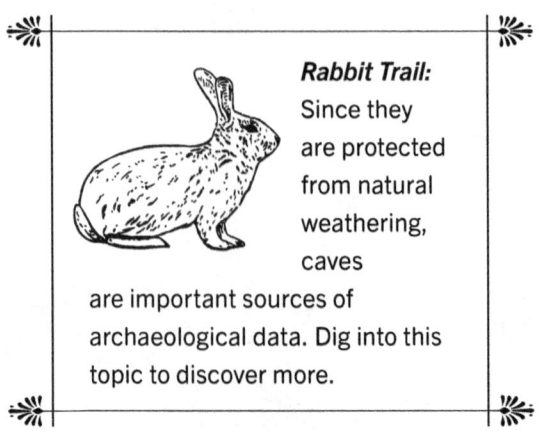

Rabbit Trail: Since they are protected from natural weathering, caves are important sources of archaeological data. Dig into this topic to discover more.

researchers to reconstruct the ancient environment and understand how it may have influenced human behavior. The cave's rock shelter and chamber offer a time capsule of human history (Harvard University, n.d.).

120,000 BCE

It's 120,000 BCE, and a couple of neat things are happening. Around this time in Eastern Africa, Homo-sapien-sapiens have emerged! We know it looks like we are rehashing old information and repeating words, but there is a distinction here; although Homo sapiens are the first actual humans we can be connected back to, Homo-sapien-sapiens (or Homo s. sapiens as we will be referring to them as from now on) are the first "modern" humans. Genetically, they are what we are today. Homo s. sapiens are thought to differ from the predecessors of Homo sapiens because of a genetic alteration in the brain that made more complicated noises possible, which allowed them to develop a language that was more complex than the previous grunting and grumbling. Give them a round of applause everyone! They can speak. Sort of... it's mostly just more intricate noises rather than actual words. See why we are so impressed by fire and rock sharpening skills now? The Homo genus wasn't even really talking yet when they were figuring that out! This absence of complicated language sure is a handicap for sharing information.

Around this time, people also made another major step. In Europe, we found evidence from this time period of fur clothes! Don't get us wrong, we are not saying the various species of humans were naked for millions of years until 120,000 BCE. Surely, people were covering the sensitive parts of their anatomy at some point before now, just for practicality's sake if for no other reason. Animal hide, however, proves the existence of a resource. The use of animal skins proves innovation.

Deer Hide, Image by JamesDeMers. Public Domain.

They were used for clothing, tent-like structures, and household items since the Paleolitic time period. Animal hides have also been used to write on, not that they were writing just yet. Animal skins were used by all species of the Homo genus, especially the Neanderthals, at this time.

The next big thing that happens around this time in the timeline is the beginning of Homo s. sapien migration out of Africa. While this happens over a large span of time, this first chunk of migration started in 120,000 BCE. Not only is that a lot of time, but it's also a lot of walking. It's not like they had an exact destination in mind or were even the same people by the time they got to their final destination. I'm sure there was a good deal of meandering and pit stops made on the way. This first chunk of migration happened long before animal **domestication** and **husbandry** were figured out, so they didn't even have help moving. So, why migrate at all if they weren't really going anywhere and didn't have a good way to get there? Well, migration is an adaptive response to fluctuating temperatures and resources. As seasons changed, animals such as birds and fish would leave cold areas for warmer ones and return when seasons changed again. People naturally followed the food and the warmth to other places. Think of animal instincts. Humans in this early period thought more like animals than modern-day people. This coincided with a glaciation period. It was cold, and they wanted out. Ironically, most of the people who tried to leave during this first wave definitely didn't make it. By that, we mean, the descendants of those people definitely died out. We just don't know how long it took for this to happen or exactly what happened to everyone. However, we do know, for example, that many of them settled in what is now the Sahara Desert when it was still fertile (Out of Africa- The Human Journey, 2023)

> **Domestication:** The slow process of altering wild plants and animals through cultivation, taming, and breeding to be used by humans.
>
> **Husbandry:** the management, cultivation, and conservation of crops and animals.

The first successful wave of migration didn't happen until...

106,000 BCE

So, this is the part where we get super-speculative. Do you remember when we established that archeology is a science that's constantly adapting to new information and getting updated regularly? Yeah, there's a lot of that happening around human migration. We have believed that the first large-scale migration attempts by Homo s. sapiens happened in 120,000 BCE; this is specifically human migration; we know other Homo genus' had already migrated at an earlier date. As I said before, it seems that this first attempt failed fantastically. At this point, we think the first successful migration happened around 106,000 BCE. This mostly makes sense since we have proof of people making it to Southern China and Europe around 90,000 BCE.

90,000 BCE

Now, we don't know why it would have taken them so long to get there, but we have to assume that it could be any number of things. Again, there was no set destination when they left and no domesticated animals to speed up the process (though there may have been boats). Obviously, this was several generations of people — not the same people walking for 16,000 years. It is likely that they settled and moved in spurts over the course of that time.

As a little break from the confusion, people were also figuring out **harpoons** around the same time. Harpoons were probably invented for fishing back in the Congo region of Africa. They were serrated and had barbed edges. Found in the Katanda site in what is currently the Democratic Republic of Congo, these tools featured early barbed points and were used to hunt huge catfish that weighed as much as 150 lbs.

Harpoon: A spear-like weapon used for hunting fish.

89,000 BCE

The second migration begins around this time and lasts until 73,000 BCE. We believe this wave continued to populate Europe and China.

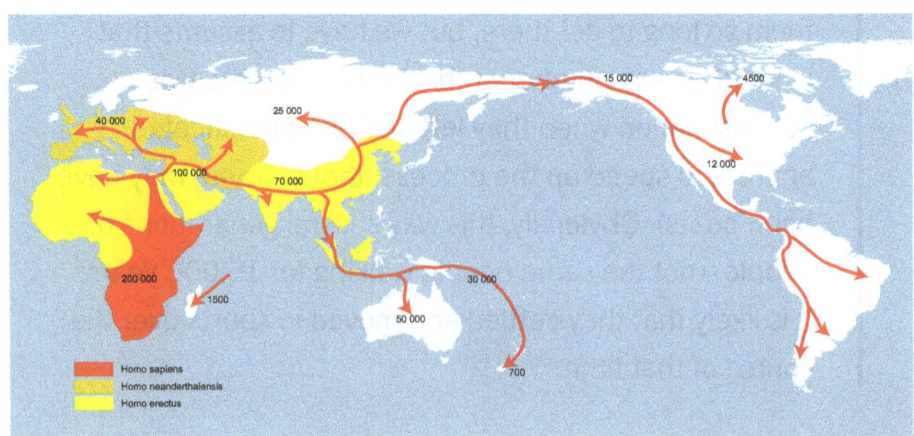

77,000 BCE

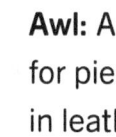

Awl: A tool used for piercing holes in leather or fabric

We believe **awls** were created in Africa. At least, the oldest one we've found so far was discovered in Africa and has been dated back to this time. Awls are basically a cross between a sewing needle and a hole punch. These were used to fashion clothing into, what we imagine was, more manageable configurations. Between the invention of the awl and fur clothing that we've found from 120,000 BCE, it seems like warmth and clothing became more of a priority around this time period. Probably due to all the ice.

61,000 BCE

A particularly interesting discovery was found in the Sibudu cave system in South Africa. Evidence of an arrow!? Sure, there were already spears, harpoons, knives, and axes at this point, but there's something exciting about the idea of the bow and arrow being invented. A bow and arrow is not only extremely recognizable today, but it is also a weapon that takes several steps to use. Unfortunately, this discovery is more of a question mark than an exclamation point. What we found were rock points. These were found with several other

advanced human tools, such as the earliest sewing needle. Look at us wearing clothes that just might fit!

At the Nataruk site in the Kenyan region of Africa, there is more evidence of bows and arrows being used. Stone-tipped arrow (or maybe spear) heads were found embedded in a human skeleton. These could be dated back as far as 71,000–61,000 BCE (Gill, 2010).

59,000 BCE

This is the third wave of migration of Homo sapiens out of Africa. It lasted around 12,000 years until about 47,000 BCE. During this migration, people started to settle in other regions of Eurasia. This is interesting because there must have been a reason that nobody inhabited the space before this. The more diverse routes and destinations for this migration wave may have had something to do with the climate. Newly arid pockets like the Horn of Africa may have spurred people to move on, while more wet, lush passages like where the Sahara Desert is today offered new routes of travel which had previously been unavailable (Timmermann & Friedrich, 2016).

45,000 BCE

This was the fourth and final wave of early migration. Interestingly, new evidence is beginning to show that at the same time people started moving out of Africa, other people may have been starting to move back into Africa around the same time. This wave lasted until around 29,000 BCE and may have been the one that populated the rest of the reachable world as well (Fang, 2019).

40,000 BCE

A link between Asian and Native American people can be dated to approximately 40,000 BCE due human remains uncovered Inside the Tianyuan Cave site near Beijing, China. Researchers found 34 fragments of human remains from one person that can be dated from 42,000–39,000 BCE, and DNA extracted from a leg bone shows that this person is likely an ancestor of present-day Asian and Native American people.

In the same period of time that this person was dying, people were learning to mine in Switzerland. This mine could technically be as old as 42,000 BCE, but we're not sure. What we do know is that hematite was unearthed in Ngwenya Mine and that this mineral was used to make red pigment for painting.

In other fire news, yeah, there's more stuff about fire. Around 40,000 BCE, we have concrete evidence of fires being made using friction to start them. That feels like a long time to figure out rubbing things together to create heat, but we have never had to invent fire.

38,000 BCE

In France, people were painting on walls. The Chauvet Cave site contains several cave paintings and animal remains that were surprisingly well preserved. This preservation condition is likely due to a rock slide that

Lions, Chauvet Cave. Public Domain.

concealed the cave from discovery for thousands of years (Hammer, 2015).

Meanwhile, people were dying in Niah Cave in Sarawak, Malaysia. Evidence of the earliest Homo sapien to date was found at the Niah Cave site, and his remains are dated back to 38,000 BCE. The Niah Cave site is one of the largest Paleolithic sites in Southeast Asia. The cave's first archaeological digging in 1954 revealed evidence of past human habitations, including flakes and chopper tools dating back to 40,000 BCE. Humans continued to live there until we figured out literacy!

The West Mouth entrance links several smaller caves and passages that lead to evidence of day-to-day human activity that lasted through prehistory. This cave site is also stuffed with rich culture and burial practices, as it seems to have been used as a burial site from 12,000 BCE all the way up until 200 BCE. This site has preserved many burial traditions and practices, such as **flexed burial, secondary jar burial, cremation,** and **supine coffin burials.**

32,000 BCE

The oldest fibers ever found were discovered in a cave in modern-day Georgia (the country in East Europe/West Asia).

Flexed Burial: A body being laid to rest in either a crouching or fetal position, with knees being pulled up to the chest.

Secondary Jar Burial: A body being laid to rest by placing the body in a large jar and then being placed in their tomb.

Cremation: A funerary ritual through which a corpse is burned

Supine Coffin Burials: A body being laid to rest face up in a casket.

We're using the term fibers here because calling what's left of it clothing or even fabric would be a reach. The fibers were made of flax and made into linen and thread, which would have been used for clothes.

Finally, we see migration to somewhere new.

30,000 BCE

In the year 30,000 BCE, something very interesting seemed to have happened. The first people may have voyaged to the Americas. Or, people may have already been there. The jury is still out.

Literature: The Epic Poem

An epic poem is a poem that recounts the trials of a semi-divine hero or someone significant to a culture's identity. These works are lengthy, narratives of poetry that often depict the extraordinary feats of heroes, the involvement of gods, and the fate of nations or peoples. They are foundational texts in many cultures, often reflecting the values, struggles, and histories of the societies from which they originate. The language of epic poetry is elevated and ceremonial, often employing literary devices such as extended similes, epithets, and formal speeches. Also, Epics often begin in the middle of the action, with earlier events recounted through flashbacks or storytelling.

The Epic of Gilgamesh

The Epic of Gilgamesh is one of the earliest known literary works, originating from ancient Mesopotamia. The story was written on a series of clay tablets in cuneiform script, a wedge-shaped writing system used by various ancient civilizations.

Researchers translated the Epic of Gilgamesh tablets uncovered in Nineveh, Iraq, by archaeologist Austen Henry Layard in the mid-19th century. These clay tablets were manufactured by pressing a wedge-shaped stylus into soft clay. Clay tablets dried after writing, preserving the narrative for decades. Tablets were stronger after baking or fire.

Synopsis: In the ancient city of Uruk, where the Euphrates River flowed and the walls rose tall and proud, there lived a mighty king named Gilgamesh. He was strong, handsome, and feared by many, but his heart longed for something more. This is the epic tale of Gilgamesh, a hero's journey filled with friendship, loss, and the quest for immortality.

Gilgamesh, a two-thirds god and one-third human, ruled over Uruk with strength and authority. However, his arrogance and disregard for his people angered the gods. In response, the gods created a wild man named Enkidu to humble Gilgamesh. At first, the two were bitter enemies, but after a fierce battle, they discovered a deep bond and became inseparable friends.

READ: Epic of Gilgamesh (version should be selected by the instructor)

Subject & Verb

The subject of a sentence is the person, place, thing, or idea that is performing the action or being described. It usually answers the questions "who?" or "what?"

- Examples:

    The **people** migrated to China.

    She harpooned a giant catfish.

    The **land** was dry and inhospitable.

The verb of a sentence is the action word or state of being. It tells what the subject does or is.

- Examples:

    The people **migrated** to China.

    She **harpooned** a giant catfish.

    The land **was** dry and inhospitable.

Contemplation: *(please answer questions in depth- answers would be 100 words or more)*

- How do we reconcile the fact that what we know about history is constantly changing?

- Choose one of the cave sites found in the chapter and write a 1-page paper about it. Use at least three sources for your supporting information. Your paper should include text from source material and links to the sources.

References

Britannica, T. Editors of Encyclopaedia (2018, May 10). *Pleistocene Series.* Encyclopedia Britannica. https://www.britannica.com/science/Pleistocene-Series

Brue, A.H. (1762). *Graeciae antiquae.* David Rumsey Historical Map Collection. https://www.davidrumsey.com/luna/servlet/s/tc6ly3

Cox, C. (2016 May 11). *Cave of Theopetra.* Flickr. https://flickr.com/photos/clairemcox/26343982853/

Fairbridge, R. W. and Agenbroad, L. D. (2024, March 29). *Holocene Epoch.* Encyclopedia Britannica. https://www.britannica.com/science/Holocene-Epoch

Fang, J. (2019, March 11). *Some humans migrated back to Africa 45,000 years ago.* IFLScience. https://www.iflscience.com/some-humans-migrated-back-africa-45000-years-ago-35937

Gill, V. (2010, August 26). *The oldest evidence of arrows found.* BBC News. https://www.bbc.com/news/science-environment-11086110

Harvard University. (n.d.). *Excavations at Theopetra Cave in Thessaly, Greece: From the Middle Paleolithic until modern times.* https://whitelevy.fas.harvard.edu/excavations-theopetra-cave-thessaly-greece-middle-paleolithic-until-modern-times

Hughes, C. (2009, August 13). *Early modern humans use fire to engineer tools from Stone.* EurekAlert! https://www.eurekalert.org/news-releases/709146

Hammer, J. (2015, April 1). *Finally, the beauty of France's Chauvet cave makes its grand public debut.* Smithsonian.com. https://www.smithsonianmag.com/history/france-chauvet-cave-makes-grand-debut-180954582/

Klein, C. (2023, September 25). *New Study Refutes Theory of How Humans Populated North America.* https://www.history.com/news/new-study-refutes-theory-of-how-humans-populated-north-america

Out of Africa. (2023, March 27). The Human Journey. https://humanjourney.us/discovering-our-distant-ancestors-section/out-of-africa/

Timmermann, A., & Friedrich, T. (2016). Late pleistocene climate drivers of early human migration. *Nature, 538*(7623), 92–95. https://doi.org/10.1038/nature19365

U.S. Department of the Interior. (n.d.). *The Bering Land Bridge theory.* National Parks Service. https://www.nps.gov/bela/learn/historyculture/the-bering-land-bridge-theory.htm

Lesson Four - More Human Behavior

Speculation:

- What is the significance of using archeology to study ancient history?

_____
_____

- What other methods of studying ancient history do we have?

_____
_____

- Consider your house or community. What one item do you see that could define your culture?

_____
_____

- What wild animal do you wish could be a pet, and why?

_____
_____

Migration

So, this is where things really get interesting when it comes to the constantly updating nature of delineating history. When we research information about how sapiens migrated to America, things get complicated rather quickly.

30,000 BCE

The most accepted theory for a long time was the Land Bridge Theory, also known as the **Bering Land Bridge.** The main idea of this theory is that around 30,000 BCE, sea levels dropped during the ongoing ice age, revealing land that connected South Siberia to Alaska and North Canada. The people who eventually became America's Indigenous population supposedly began migrating across the bridge by 16,500 BCE and made it south of the Canadian ice sheets by 15,000 BCE. However, this is far from certain, as newer evidence shows that this path to the Americas may not have been as viable as we once believed.

Eske Willerslev, an evolutionary geneticist who led the first successful **sequencing** of ancient **DNA**, and

Bering Land Bridge: A piece of land that once connected Siberia and North America.

DNA Sequencing: Determining the order of something's genetic material.

DNA: Deoxyribonucleic acid is a chain of nucleotides, present in most living organisms, that creates a structure that carries the genetic material.

his colleagues have published a series of studies that have fundamentally changed how we think about human history (Klein, 2018) (Zimmer, 2016). The researchers studied the pollen, macrofossils, and DNA from lake sediments found within the Peace River Basin, an important section of the proposed migration path over the Bering Land Bridge. The research results found that the **corridor's choke point** was not "biologically viable" enough to have sustained humans on the arduous journey until 12,600 years ago—centuries after people were known to have been in North America. Willerslev's team found that until that time the bottleneck area lacked the basic necessities for survival, such as wood for fuel and tools or game animals to be killed for sustenance by hunter-gatherers (Deslilva, 2022). This shows that while the land bridge existed at some point, it would not have been a feasible pathway for the first people who migrated to the continent. In fact, Anthropological Geneticist

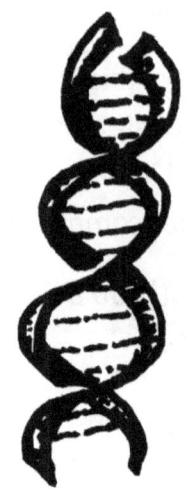

Corridor's Choke Point: A narrow passageway that leaves little to no room for other flow of traffic or alternate routes.

Kelp Highway Hypothesis: Theory that the first Americans arrived by boat rather than on foot, following the kelp rich Pacific coastline from northeastern Asia and Beringia to as far south as South America.

Jennifer Raff has compiled information showing America having been inhabited much longer than scientists have presumed for the last several centuries. Her book, *Origin: A Genetic History of the Americas*, shows "well-dated archaeological sites, including recently announced 22,000-year-old human footprints from White Sands, New Mexico, are at odds with the Clovis first hypothesis" (Klein, 2023). (We'll talk more about that later). Raff uses archaeological and genetic evidence to argue that the path prehistoric humans used to reach the Americas was coastal instead of on land (the Kelp Highway Hypothesis). She goes on to argue that Beringia was not a bridge, rather a sizable settlement region used for millennia by ancestors of indigenous Americans.

So, now We've introduced a new term: **The Kelp Highway Hypothesis**. The article *The Kelp Highway Hypothesis: Marine Ecology, the Coastal Migration Theory, and the Peopling of the Americas* in the Journal of Island & Coastal Archaeology discusses several of the earliest archaeological sites which are on islands and along the coastline near resource rich kelp forests.  The animal remains found in these sites are shellfish, fish, and sea mammals which reinforces the idea that the people were using the kelp forest to forage for food. Between 18,000 and 13,000 years ago, a linear band of productive kelp forests may have extended from Japan to Baja California, providing a "kelp highway" to facilitate maritime peoples' migration into the New World (Erlandson, et. al., 2007). This theory, as well as other land bridge alternative theories, are all far from being proven. Which simply goes to show that we still don't know everything about human history, even when it comes to the things we thought we've known since the 1800's.

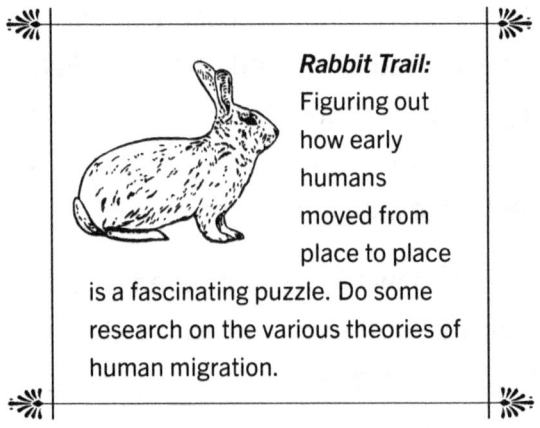

Rabbit Trail: Figuring out how early humans moved from place to place is a fascinating puzzle. Do some research on the various theories of human migration.

30,000 BCE

In entirely unrelated news, people in the Xiaoshan, Liaoning Province of China were making sewing needles from bone. We know that feels anticlimactic, especially since we've already discussed the invention of sewing needles literally tens of thousands of years earlier, but trust us, this is important. This is a sign that we are approaching the Mesolithic period, even as early as 30,000 BCE, when that period of the Stone Age won't officially start for another 20,000 years. The Mesolithic period was a time of cultural development and diversification, so the evidence of upgraded versions of a tool specialized to a certain region shows development in this direction. These needles were used primarily to make warm garments. This, combined with the waves of large migrations to other regions of the world, just goes to show how sick people were of being cold... or dying from extremely low temperatures. We were in an ice age after all.

28,000 BCE

Continuing with the trend of early advancements, in what is now the modern day Czech Republic, we have found the earliest recorded evidence of clay being used to make stuff. At Dolni Vestonice, a prominent archaeological site, figurines made of clay mixed with crushed mammoth bone have been uncovered. These figurines were made and fired as a form of artistic expression (see, we're still finding uses for fires). This is interesting because not only does it say a lot about human mental development, it also means that people are beginning to have time for artistic expression. It must have been a nice change to be able to divert energy from basic survival to **cathartic** hobbies.

Cathartic: Involving the release of strong emotions through a particular activity or experience.

25,000 BCE

Fertility seems to be important to the people of this time period. In the remains of the campsite St. Germain-en-

Figure from Hacilar. Public Domain.

Laye in France, early clay sculptures depicting pregnant women were found. Hacilar, a prehistoric town in Turkey, had depictions of women as goddesses. The cave site, Catalhyuk, had images suggesting that oracles or cult priestesses were being **venerated** at the time. These early artistic depictions of women were dominated by full figured forms. What is most interesting about these figurines is that they were tiny. By all indications they were meant to be worn. This signifies some kind of veneration or possible worship status.

Meanwhile, in Spain, paintings were found from two periods of human occupation at the Altamira cave site. People from the **Gravettian** group, who inhabited large areas across Europe, lived in this cave from 25,000–20,000 BCE and people from the **Middle Magdalenian**, living in Central Europe and northern Spain, inhabited it from 15,000–10,000 BCE. Numerous archaeological remains were left behind by these groups (Kozlowski et.al., 2014) (Alvarez, 2022).

Venerated: To admire, worship, honor, give devotion, or regard reverently.

Gravettian: A paleolithic culture found throughout Europe following the Aurignacian period of migration out of Africa characterized by a blade tool with a narrow point and blunt back edge (Merriam-Webster, n.d.).

Middle Magdalenian: A culture from the Upper Paleolithic period in Europe known for their artistically engraved designs on their weapons, tools, and ornaments (Britannica, 2023).

17,000 BCE

In 17,000 BCE, weaponry was becoming more advanced in France. The invention of the **atlatl**, a simple tool that assisted in launching spears by hand, is pretty impressive. This tool basically used leverage to gain velocity when throwing darts or spears. Sort of like how you use a lacrosse stick to throw balls farther and faster, except it's much smaller, made of wood or bone with a hook, and launches A SPEAR, which is much cooler (Hirst, 2019).

Atlatl: A spear-throwing tool using leverage to achieve greater distance.

15,000 BCE

Sticking to France, the Lascaux cave site has about 600 paintings and around 1,500 engravings from human occupation. Like many other caves, archaeologists believe that it was a center for hunting and **religious rites**. Like a prehistoric

Religious Rite: A traditional ceremony or ritual done for religious purposes.

town square or community center, people gathered here for community activities such as food processing, eating, and religious practices (History.com Editors, 2020).

Bull and Horses, Lascaux Cave. Licensed by Adobe Stock.

A different cave site in America located in modern-day Austin, Texas, is called Buttermilk Creek, which is a very Southern American name for a place. This site was found fairly recently in 2006 and dates back to 15,000 BCE. It was originally labeled as one of the **Clovis sites**, which will come up a couple of times in

Clovis Culture: A culture of people in North America known for distinctive spearheads.

Pre-Clovis: Things in the Americas that are dated to be older than the artifacts found at the Clovis archaeological site.

Clovis Points, Image by Watts. Licensed under Creative Commons 2.0 BY.

upcoming chapters. An odd thing that happened with multiple cave sites, including ones we've mentioned earlier, is that for a while, tourists and the general populace were allowed to just play around in the caves as if they weren't important archaeological findings. This was usually done for educational purposes after scientists thought they'd found all that they were going to be able to find, which is good, but damaging to the historical conservation, which is not so great. In fact, the Buttermilk Creek site was a pay-to-dig attraction for a period of time. This one, like many others, was eventually closed to the public and became solely accessible to academic researchers. In this case, that was especially good because it resulted in archaeologists finding a literal trove of **pre-Clovis** artifacts, which ended up reshaping the way American archaeologists approached the digs; they actively contradicted the Clovis First Model of archeology, which, again, we'll be addressing in later chapters (Waters et. al., 2018).

Similarly, The Monte Verde site in modern day Chile is a very important discovery in the Americas. This site was found in 1975 by locals after discovering large animal bones uncovered by erosion of the creek's bank. During excavation, they discovered a good number of extremely well preserved Pre-Clovis artifacts including "food scraps from megafauna and wads of masticated seaweed, likely chewed for medicinal purposes." (Alex, 2019).

In less groundbreaking but equally exciting news: around the same time, people were beginning to domesticate animals. Specifically wolves. That's right, everybody! Dogs are just over the horizon! DOGS, DOGS, DOGS! Everything else that has happened in this chapter is interesting, but the promise of dogs is objectively our favorite... other than the spear launchers, those are also pretty great.

14,500 BCE

In Japan, they were now developing a very distinctive method of pottery decoration. Beginning in the **Jōmon Period** from 14,500–300 BCE, the Japanese were making vessels with rope designs and details. The word "Jōmon" means cord pattern, thus the name. At this point, the population still wasn't practicing agriculture; clay pots and vessels were being used to prepare food, so they were not quite decorative yet, although decoration was starting to be added.

Jōmon Period: The Neolithic period of Japan characterized by distinctive pottery (Merriam-Webster, n.d.).

Jōmon Period Pottery, Image by Gary Todd. Public Domain.

>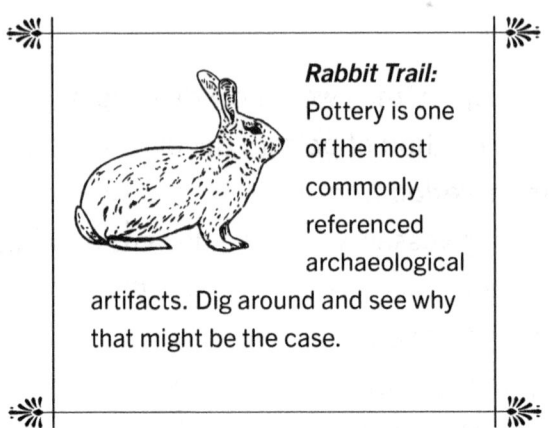
> **Rabbit Trail:** Pottery is one of the most commonly referenced archaeological artifacts. Dig around and see why that might be the case.

14,000 BCE

This is the beginning of the end of an era, literally. While both the Paleolithic Period and the Ice Age were beginning to wind down, this is far from the actual end of the Stone Age. As we discussed earlier, the Paleolithic Period was followed by two more periods before we reached the beginning of the Metal Ages. However, we have reached the end of the period ruled by periods of glaciation. The end of the Ice Age signals the beginning of a different way of life for human populations. Imagine the burden of strangely fluctuating warm and cold patterns suddenly lifting and leaving you with more predictable weather patterns. You now have the luxury of being able to plan for not only the next ten years, but larger chunks of you and your children's lives. It changes everything!

 Watch these Videos: Theories of Human Migration Part I
http://link.cheesepresspublishing.com/migrationOne
Theories of Human Migration Part II
http://link.cheesepresspublishing.com/migrationTwo

Literature: The Genesis Creation Story

The oldest stories are creation stories. As long as there have been people, they have tried to figure out the secrets of the world and their place in it. Myths about creation try to explain how the world, people, and God came to be. Creation stories tend to have similar themes and patterns, even if they are told in different languages, cultures, and places. These include the role of a divine creator, the fight between chaos and order, and the birth of humanity.

You should be reading the Epic of Gilgamesh right now. While it is an epic poem, it has many of the elements of a creation story. There are some striking similarities between Gilgamesh and the creation story found in Genesis.

The Book of Genesis

The texts of Abrahamic religions (Judaism, Christianity, and Islam) are other ancient works of literature. The Book of Genesis, the first book of the Christian Old Testament, is a complex literary work that has significantly influenced Western literature and culture. It is a narrative text with interconnected stories, tracing the creation of the world, the early history of humanity, and the lives of key patriarchs. The narrative structure follows a chronological order, with symbolism and allegory used to convey these ideas. The theme of creation and covenant is central, presenting a narrative depicting God as the ultimate Creator. The basic elements of the story found in the Christian interpretations of Genesis are also found in the Jewish Torah and the Muslim Quran.

Excerpt:

Genesis 2: Thus the heavens and the earth were completed in all their vast array.

2 By the seventh day God had finished the work he had been doing; so on the seventh day he rested from all his work. 3 Then God blessed the seventh day and made it holy, because on it he rested from all the work of creating that he had done.

Adam and Eve

4 This is the account of the heavens and the earth when they were created, when the Lord God made the earth and the heavens.

5 Now no shrub had yet appeared on the earth and no plant had yet sprung up, for the Lord God had not sent rain on the earth and there was no one to work the ground, 6 but streams came up from the earth and watered the whole surface of the ground. 7 Then the Lord God formed a man from the dust of the ground and breathed into his nostrils the breath of life, and the man became a living being.

8 Now the Lord God had planted a garden in the east, in Eden; and there he put the man he had formed. 9 The Lord God made all kinds of trees grow out of the ground—trees that were pleasing to the eye and good for food. In the middle of the garden were the tree of life and the tree of the knowledge of good and evil.

10 A river watering the garden flowed from Eden; from there it was separated into four headwaters. 11 The name of the first is the Pishon; it winds through the entire land of Havilah, where there is gold. 12 (The gold of that land is good; aromatic resin and onyx are also there.) 13 The name of the second river is the Gihon; it winds through the entire land of Cush. 14 The name of the third river is the Tigris; it runs along the east side of Ashur. And the fourth river is the Euphrates.

15 The Lord God took the man and put him in the Garden of Eden to work it and take care of it. 16 And the Lord God commanded the man, "You are free to eat from any tree in the garden; 17 but you must not eat from the tree of the knowledge of good and evil, for when you eat from it you will certainly die."

18 The Lord God said, "It is not good for the man to be alone. I will make a helper suitable for him."

19 Now the Lord God had formed out of the ground all the wild animals and all the birds in the sky. He brought them to the man to see what he would name them; and whatever the man called each living creature, that was its name. 20 So the man gave names to all the livestock, the birds in the sky and all the wild animals.

But for Adam no suitable helper was found. 21 So the Lord God caused the man to fall into a deep sleep; and while he was sleeping, he took one of the man's ribs and then closed up the place with flesh. 22 Then the Lord God made a woman from the rib he had taken out of the man, and he brought her to the man.

23 The man said,

"This is now bone of my bones

    and flesh of my flesh;

she shall be called 'woman,'

    for she was taken out of man."

24 That is why a man leaves his father and mother and is united to his wife, and they become one flesh.

25 Adam and his wife were both naked, and they felt no shame.

(New International Version Bible, Gen 2)

Contemplation: *(please answer questions in depth- answers would be 100 words or more)*

- What are the different hypotheses on how early man got to the Americas?

- Which hypothesis seems more likely? Why?

- What do creation myths tell us about ancient man? Give a reason as to why you think there are similarities in these myths.

References

Alex, B. (2019, November 19). *Monte Verde: Our earliest evidence of humans living in South America.* Discover Magazine. https://www.discovermagazine.com/planet-earth/monte-verde-our-earliest-evidence-of-humans-living-in-south-america

Alvarez, S. (2022, April 3). *Altamira cave.* Ancient Art Archive. https://www.ancientartarchive.org/altamira-cave-spain/

Britannica, T. Editors of Encyclopaedia (2023, October 11). *Magdalenian culture.* Encyclopedia Britannica. https://www.britannica.com/topic/Magdalenian-culture

Desilva, J. (2022, February 8). *Did the first Americans arrive via land bridge? this geneticist says no.* The New York Times. https://www.nytimes.com/2022/02/08/books/review/A-Genetic-History-of-the-Americas-By-Jennifer-Raff.html

Erlandson, J. M., Graham, M. H., Bourque, B. J., Corbett, D., Estes, J. A., & Steneck, R. S. (2007). The Kelp Highway Hypothesis: Marine ecology, the Coastal Migration Theory, and the peopling of the Americas. *The Journal of Island and Coastal Archaeology, 2*(2), 161–174. https://doi.org/10.1080/15564890701628612

Hirst, K. K. (2019, May 30). *The technology and history of the atlatl spear thrower.* ThoughtCo. https://www.thoughtco.com/what-is-an-atlatl-169989

History.com Editors. (2020, September 10). *Lascaux cave paintings discovered.* History. https://www.history.com/this-day-in-history/lascaux-cave-paintings-discovered

Klein, C. (2018, August 29). *New Study refutes theory of how humans populated North America.* History.com. https://www.history.com/news/new-study-refutes-theory-of-how-humans-populated-north-america

Kozłowski, J. K., Moreau, L., Adam, E., Aubry, T.,... Klíma, B. (2014, April 8). The origin of the Gravettian. *Quaternary International.* https://www.sciencedirect.com/science/article/abs/pii/S1040618214001621#:~:text=The%20Gravettian%20is%20an%20Upper,be%20placed%20on%20various%20levels.

Merriam-Webster. (n.d.). *Gravettian.* In Merriam-Webster.com dictionary. https://www.merriam-webster.com/dictionary/Gravettian

Merriam-Webster. (n.d.). *Jomon.* In Merriam-Webster.com dictionary. Retrieved July 20, 2024, from https://www.merriam-webster.com/dictionary/jomon

Waters, M. R., Keene, J. L., Forman, S. L., Prewitt, E. R., Carlson, D. L., & Wiederhold, J. E. (2018). Pre-Clovis projectile points at the Debra L. Friedkin site, Texas — Implications for the Late Pleistocene peopling of the Americas. *American Association for the Advancement of Science*, 1–13.

Zimmer, C. (2016, May 16). *Eske Willerslev is rewriting history with DNA.* The New York Times. https://www.nytimes.com/2016/05/17/science/eske-willerslev-ancient-dna-scientist.html

Andrea Hermitt

Andrea Hermitt is a co-founder of Cheese Press Publishing and one of the authors of the Cheese Press History curriculum. Andrea earned an art degree in 1991 from State University of New York at Albany, and furthered her education by earning a Master's of Education from the University of the People in 2023.

As a homeschooling parent of now adult children, Andrea has been deeply involved in education for many years. Since 2019, she has served as a Homeschool Program Director, where she combines her extensive knowledge and experience to support and guide other homeschooling families.

Andrea's background in art and education, coupled with her hands-on experience in homeschooling, brings a unique and valuable perspective to her writing. Her dedication to learning and teaching is evident in her contributions to the Cheese Press History series, where she expertly blends historical insight with engaging narratives.

Andrea Hermitt's multifaceted expertise and passion for education make her a key contributor to the collaborative process of bringing this world history series to life. Her perspective offers readers a rich and well-rounded understanding of any topic she explores.

Jordan Hermitt ~

Jordan Hermitt, co-author on *An Introduction to the Study of History* is known for her diverse talents and rich educational background. Homeschooled from grades 3 through 12, Jordan developed a profound appreciation for history and learning early on. She graduated from Wesleyan College in 2017 at the age of 20, showcasing her academic excellence and passion for knowledge.

As a playwright, theatre artist, and costumer, Jordan brings a unique perspective to her writing, blending creativity with meticulous research. She brings her talent for depth of knowledge and vivid storytelling to the table as co-author of a Cheese Press History.

In addition to her artistic pursuits, Jordan is a dedicated homeschool instructor, sharing her love for history and the arts with her students. Her multifaceted background and commitment to education make her an invaluable contributor to the field of historical literature. Jordan Hermitt's expertise and passion for history promise to bring new insights and engaging narratives to readers everywhere.

Check out the introductory text for this series:
AN INTRODUCTION TO THE STUDY OF HISTORY

Designed primarily for high school students, this comprehensive guide is also invaluable for adults seeking to discover a new passion for historical study. This book is a precursor to a Cheese Press History's four year world history curriculum, providing a solid foundation for deeper exploration. Readers will gain insights into the methods historians use to study the past, learn to critically analyze historical sources, and understand the interconnectedness of global events. Whether you are a student preparing for an advanced history course or an adult returning to the study of history, this book offers the tools and knowledge needed to navigate the vast and fascinating landscape of world history. Discover the past, understand the present, and prepare for a more informed future with *An Introduction to the Study of History* by Mere Jones and Jordan Hermitt.

VEINS OF CIVILIZATION: ANCIENT HISTORY

Veins of Civilization is a dynamic and engaging textbook series designed to help students explore the rich and interconnected story of human history. Students learn that history is more than a list of conflicts; it is a series of cause-and-effect events that, when taught in order, reveals a rich narrative that they can relate to.

Each collection in this series offers a captivating and comprehensive journey through different historical periods, highlighting the foundational elements and transformative events that have shaped our world.

The series features four collections of books, with each collection chronicling a different historical era over 28 lessons. The course of study covers ancient, medieval, early modern, and modern history periods and are intended to be consumed in chronological order.

Veins of Civilization: Ancient History

The first collection introduces students to the origins of early civilizations. From the first evidence of man to the fall of the Western Roman Empire, this book explores how early societies developed and interacted, setting the stage for the ravages of Medieval History.

Book Two - September 2024

www.ingramcontent.com/pod-product-compliance
Lightning Source LLC
Chambersburg PA
CBHW070549090426
42735CB00013B/3129